The Story of

The Great Fire of London

Anita Ganeri

 Raintree

www.raintreepublishers.co.uk
Visit our website to find out more information about **Raintree** books.

To order:
☎ Phone 44 (0) 1865 888112
🖹 Send a fax to 44 (0) 1865 314091
💻 Visit the Raintree Bookshop at **www.raintreepublishers.co.uk** to browse our catalogue and order online.

First published in Great Britain by Raintree, Halley Court, Jordan Hill, Oxford OX2 8EJ, part of Pearson Education. Raintree is a registered trademark of Pearson Education Ltd.

© Pearson Education Ltd 2008
The moral right of the proprietor has been asserted.

Editorial: Sian Smith
Design: Kimberley R. Miracle, Big Top and
 Joanna Hinton-Malivoire
Picture research: Ruth Blair
Production: Duncan Gilbert
Illustrated by Beehive Illustration
Originated by Dot Gradations

Printed and bound in China by Leo Paper Group

ISBN 978 14062 1010 1 (hardback)
ISBN 978 14062 1020 0 (paperback)

12 11 10 09 08
10 9 8 7 6 5 4 3 2 1

British Library Cataloguing in Publication Data
Ganeri, Anita, 1961-
  The story of the Great Fire of London
  1. Great Fire, London, England, 1666 -
Juvenile literature
  2. London (England) - History - 17th century
- Juvenile literature
  I. Title
  942.1'2066

Acknowledgments
The publishers would like to thank the following for permission to reproduce photographs: ©Alamy pp.14 (Lebrecht Music and Arts Photo Library), 18 (Visual Arts Library, London); ©The Art Archive p.12 (London Museum, Eileen Tweedy) ©Bridgeman Art Library pp.10 (Private Collection), 5 (The Trustees of the Goodwood Collection); ©Corbis p.19 (Michael Nicholson); ©Getty Images pp.4 (Time & Life Pictures); ©istockphoto.com p.17; ©source unknown p9.

Cover photograph reproduced with permission of © Bridgeman Art Library (Yale Center for British Art, Paul Mellon Collection, USA).

Every effort has been made to contact copyright holders of any material reproduced in this book. Any omissions will be rectified in subsequent printings if notice is given to the publisher.

Disclaimer
All the Internet addresses (URLs) given in this book were valid at the time of going to press. However, due to the dynamic nature of the Internet, some addresses may have changed, or sites may have changed or ceased to exist since publication. While the author and publisher regret any inconvenience this may cause readers, no responsibility for any such changes can be accepted by either the author or the publisher.

Contents

Some words are printed in bold, **like this**. You can find out what they mean in the glossary.

What was the Great Fire of London?

This picture was made by Samuel Rolle who was alive at the time of the Great Fire. Colour was added to it after he made it.

A very long time ago, a fire destroyed the old city of London. The fire was so big that it was called the Great Fire of London. The fire spread very quickly and burned down thousands of buildings. After the fire, the city had to be **rebuilt**.

King Charles II dressed in the clothes of the Stuart age.

The Great Fire of London happened in the year 1666. At that time, King Charles II was the king of England. King Charles belonged to the Stuart family, so this time was known as the Stuart **age**.

Fire! Fire!

The Great Fire of London started in a **bakery** in a street called Pudding Lane. It was early in the morning on Sunday 2 September 1666. One of the workers in the bakery woke the baker up. The worker could smell smoke. A fire had started!

Soon the flames were roaring fiercely. The
baker and his family were trapped upstairs. The
smoke was getting thicker. They had to escape
quickly. They opened a window and climbed on
to the roof. Then they jumped to safety on to
the roof next door.

The fire spreads

The Great Fire started as a small fire, but it spread very quickly. This is because there was a strong wind, which blew the flames from one building to another. Soon the fire was out of control.

This model shows us what streets and houses looked like at the time of the Great Fire.

There was another reason why the fire spread so quickly. At the time of the Great Fire, houses were built with wooden frames. They were called **timber-framed** houses. Sparks from the fire set the wooden buildings alight. The wood burned easily. Many houses had roofs made from **thatch**. The thatch also caught fire easily.

Trying to escape

This was painted by Lieve Verschuier who was alive at the time of the Great Fire.

Soon hundreds of houses were burning. The smoke from the fire was thick and black. People were very frightened. They wanted to get to safety. Some people went down to the River Thames to catch a boat across to the other side. Other people tried to escape from the city in carts.

Some people sheltered in churches. They took their furniture and belongings with them. They hoped that the churches would not catch fire because the walls were made from stone. But many of the churches also burned down.

Fighting the fire

This bucket was used during the Great Fire in 1666. It can still be seen today.

Today, firefighters have special machinery to help them put out fires. They have fire engines to carry their ladders and hoses. At the time of the Great Fire, there was no **fire brigade** to call. People tried to put out the flames with buckets of water. They had to carry the water from the River Thames. It took a long time and did not stop the fire.

People also pulled down burning buildings with **firehooks**. They hoped that this would stop the fire from spreading. But the fire was too strong and it carried on burning.

The fire ends

Etiam periere Ruinæ

W. Hollar fecit A° 1666

This picture shows St Paul's Cathedral on fire. It was made by someone who was alive at the time.

On Tuesday 4 September, St Paul's **Cathedral** burned down. It was the most famous building in London. Everyone thought that the cathedral was safe because it had thick, stone walls. But it was covered in wooden **scaffolding** because it was being repaired. The scaffolding caught fire. The cathedral was quickly destroyed.

The next day, the wind stopped and the fire began to go out. It had been burning for four days. The king ordered his soldiers to blow up the buildings closest to the flames. This also helped to stop the fire spreading.

London in ruins

After the Great Fire, the city of London was in **ruins**. The fire burned more than 13,000 houses to the ground. Not many people died, but many people lost their homes. They had to shelter in huts or tents. People in other parts of England sent money to help them.

St Paul's Cathedral today.

London had to be **rebuilt**. A man called Christopher Wren planned a new city. This time, he built houses using stone and brick so that they could not catch fire easily. He also built a new St Paul's **Cathedral**. You can see it in London today.

17

How do we know about the Great Fire?

This is a painting of Samuel Pepys.

Some famous writers lived in London at the time of the Great Fire. Their names were Samuel Pepys and John Evelyn. They were **eyewitnesses** to the fire. This means that they saw the fire actually happening. They wrote about the fire in their **diaries**. Their diaries tell us what happened.

This monument to the Great Fire stands in London today.

There are also lots of paintings and pictures which show what the Great Fire might have looked like. This **monument** was built near Pudding Lane where the fire started. Christopher Wren **designed** it to remind people of the Great Fire.

Teachers' guide

These books have followed the QCA guidelines closely, but space has not allowed us to cover all the information and vocabulary the QCA suggest. Any suggested material not covered in the book is added to the discussion points below. The books can simply be read as information books, or they could be used as a focus for studying the unit. Below are discussion points grouped in pairs of pages, with suggested follow-up activities.

PAGES 4–5

Talk about:

- Display some pictures of modern London and discuss what the buildings are made of. Explain that, a long time ago, the buildings in London were mostly timber-framed. Many had tiled roofs, but some (especially the poor parts) had thatched roofs, even though there was a law forbidding them because of the fire risk. Tell them that, during the Stuart period, there was a huge fire that lasted for several days. Show them a picture of the monument to the fire (page 19) and say it is still there now. Explain who Charles II was, and who Pepys was.

Possible activity:

- Mark the Stuart period in Britain on the class timeline and mark the year of the Great Fire.

- Look at the pictures of Charles II on page 5 and Samuel Pepys on page 18. Find at least four things that show they come from the Stuart period, not our own.

PAGES 6–7

Talk about:

- Discuss why the fire broke out. There were often fires in the city, but they usually only affected a few streets and were quickly put out. In Stuart times, there was no electricity, so cooking was done in ovens and over fires. There was a law saying all people had to make sure that all their fires were out at night. No one knows exactly why this fire got out of control and spread from the enclosed oven to the house.

Possible activity:

- Play http://www.tes.co.uk/greatfire/fire.html which gives a good, quick summary (after you register).

- Brainstorm the words and sounds that go with a fire burning: roaring, crackling, flames, sparks, smoke, belching, burning. Write a poem about waking to find there is a fire near by.

PAGES 8–9

Talk about:

- Remind the children about houses being made from timber. Explain that they were also crowded together and so fire could spread from one to the other very easily. There were warehouses nearby, full of things that burned easily. Say that very few lives were lost, because people could get out in time, ahead of the fire. Explain that this fire got so out of control because the wind was blowing very strongly, and did so for days.

Possible activity:

- Make a simple spider diagram of the reasons why the fire spread so quickly.

PAGES 10–11

Talk about:

- Explain that there were no banks: everything people had was in their home. Homes were not insured. If you left your home and the fire didn't reach it, you might get back to find the possessions you didn't carry away were stolen. Rich people filled their carriages with their most valuable things. Some people managed to hire boats or carts, but there were not enough of them for the people trying to escape. Pepys buried a large, expensive cheese and lots of bottles of wine in his garden when he decided to leave his home.

Possible activity:

• Role play: it is the second day of the fire. The air is full of black smoke and the fire is moving towards your home. Have a family discussion about when to leave.

PAGES 12–13

Talk about:

• Discuss how modern fires are put out and how modern firefighters get water. Explain that this was very different in Stuart times. One of the biggest differences is that there was no one really in charge of fighting fires, usually the local people all worked together to put out the smaller ones. Once it was out of control the lord mayor tried to stop it but he told Pepys: *"the people will not obey me"*. How do people get hold of the firefighters today?

Possible activity:

• Make a comparison chart between then and now for fighting fires. Some points of comparison to use could be: calling firefighters; who is in charge; trained firefighters; types of equipment; access to water.

PAGES 14–15

Talk about:

• Explain that the blowing up of buildings closest to the flames made a gap the fire couldn't cross. King Charles didn't order this to be done until the fire had burned St Paul's and was getting close to the Tower of London (which belonged to the King and also had gunpowder in it). Discuss why he acted when he did.

Possible activity:

• Mark the events of the fire, day by day, on a timeline.

PAGES 16–17

Talk about:

• Explain that London, although one of the biggest cities in the world in Stuart times, was much smaller than it is today. Discuss what you would need to rebuild the city. What lessons would you learn from the fire in terms of building materials, width of the streets and so on?

Possible activity:

• Use the map at http://www.luminarium.org/encyclopedia/greatfire.htm to mark the extent of the fire on a modern map.

PAGES 18–19

Talk about:

• Talk about the importance of eyewitnesses when finding out about things that happened in the past. Either now, or at the various points in the book where they match the events, you could read extracts from Pepys about the fire. They can be found at http://www.pepys.info/fire.html.

Possible activity:

• Use http://www.bbc.co.uk/schools/famouspeople/standard/pepys/learn/index.shtml#focus to make a timeline of Pepys' life.

Possible visit

The Museum of London has an exhibition on the Great Fire of London (more details at http://www.museumoflondon.org.uk/English/EventsExhibitions/Special/LondonsBurning/)

Find out more

Books

Great Events: The Great Fire of London, Gillian Clements (Franklin Watts, 2001)

How Do We Know About…? The Great Fire of London, Deborah Fox (Heinemann Library, 2002)

Start-up History: The Great Fire of London, Stewart Ross (Evans Brothers, 2002)

Websites

www.bbc.co.uk/history/british/civil_war_revolution/launch_ani_ fire_london.shtml
The animation on this site shows London's skyline before and after the Great Fire.

www.museumoflondon.org.uk/English/EventsExhibitions/Special/ LondonsBurning/
Explore the Great Fire of London and find out how it shaped London today.

Places to visit

St Paul's Cathedral, London

The Great Fire Monument, London

The Museum of London.

Glossary

age length of time in history

bakery shop where bread is made and cooked

cathedral large and important church

designed made in a special way

diaries books in which people write down what happens each day

eyewitnesses people who see something happen

fire brigade people and equipment used to fight fires

firehooks long hooks used to pull burning buildings down

monument building or statue built to remember someone or something

rebuilt when something is built again after it has been destroyed

ruins destroyed, or the remains of badly-damaged buildings

scaffolding frame of wooden or metal poles put up around a building while it is being repaired

thatch straw or reeds used to cover a roof

timber-framed houses houses with a frame made from wood

Index